....

I0790869

....

NOW SIGN. CAN'T SIGN? STAMP YOUR HAND!

TAKE ADVANTAGE OF THIS ALMOST
EMPTY PAGE AND DRAW SOMENTING!

TO CARO

BECAUSE SHE NEEDS IT

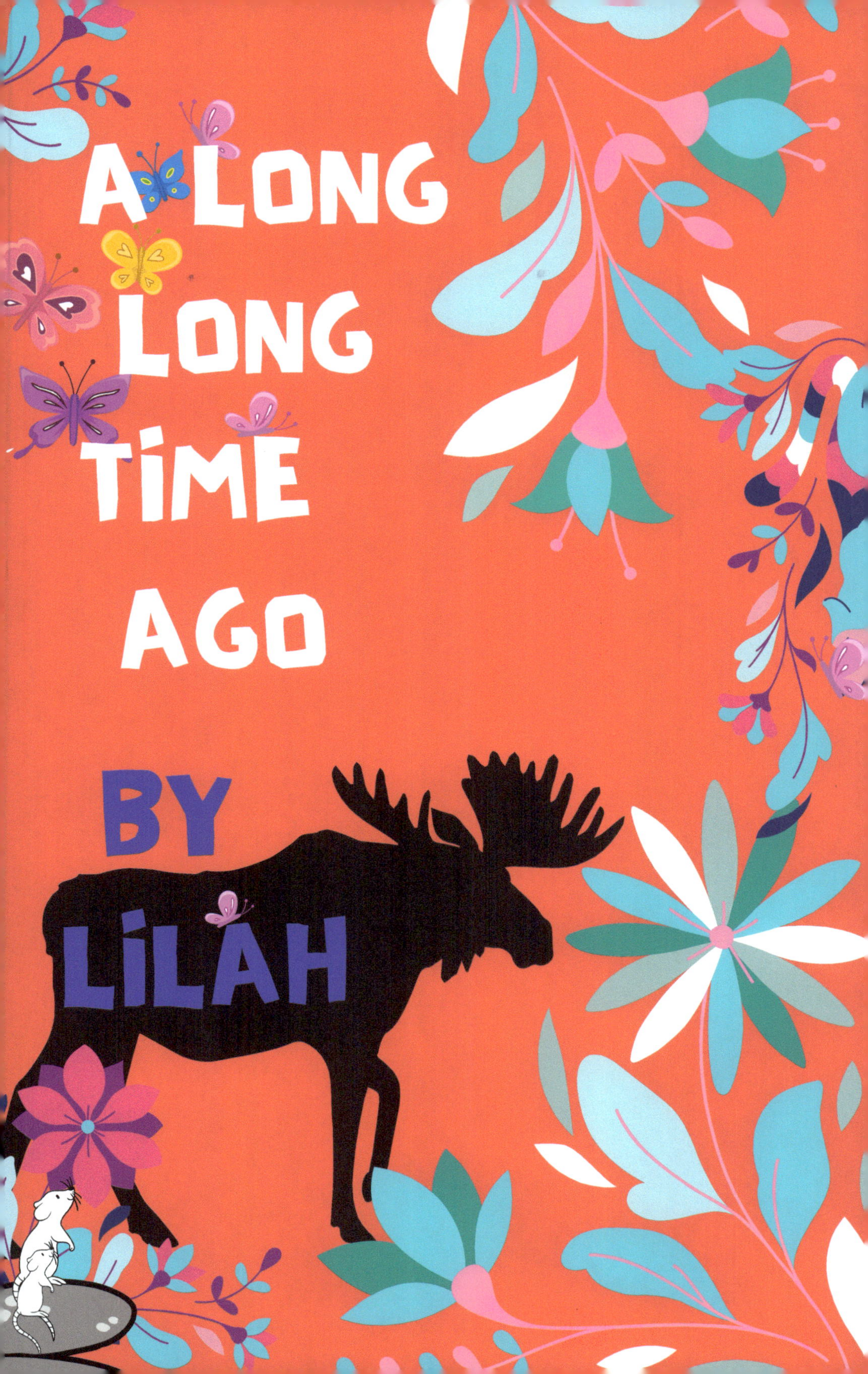

A LONG LONG TIME AGO
BY LILAH

YOU KNOW WHAT I THINK ABOUT BLANK PAGES...

A LONG LONG TIME AGO THERE WAS NO ICE CREAM

CAN YOU IMAGINE A WORLD
WITHOUT ICE CREAM?
I CAN'T!

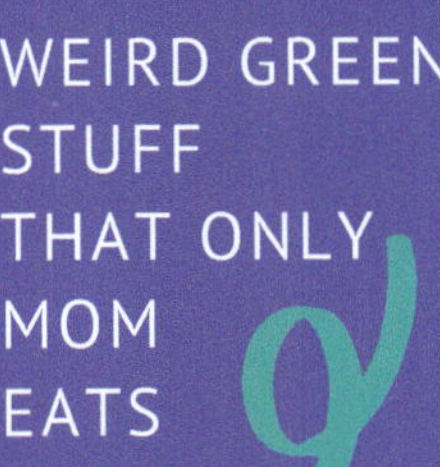

A LONG LONG TIME AGO

THERE WERE NO CARS...

SO YOU HAD TO WALK EVERYWHERE. REALLY? WALK?

NO ICE CREAM AND NO CARS I'M NOT LIKING THIS STORY!

ice cream • ice cream • ice cream • ice cream

A LONG TIME AGO THERE WERE NO CITIES, NO BUILDINGS, NO STORES....

AND NO CONTAMINATION OR SMOG

NO SMOG? FINALLY SOMETHING I KIND OF LIKE

REALLY NO STORES? WHERE DID PEOPLE A LONG TIME AGO BUY THEIR FOOD?

SUCH A GOOD QUESTION! THAT'S WHAT I WANTED TO TELL YOU TODAY

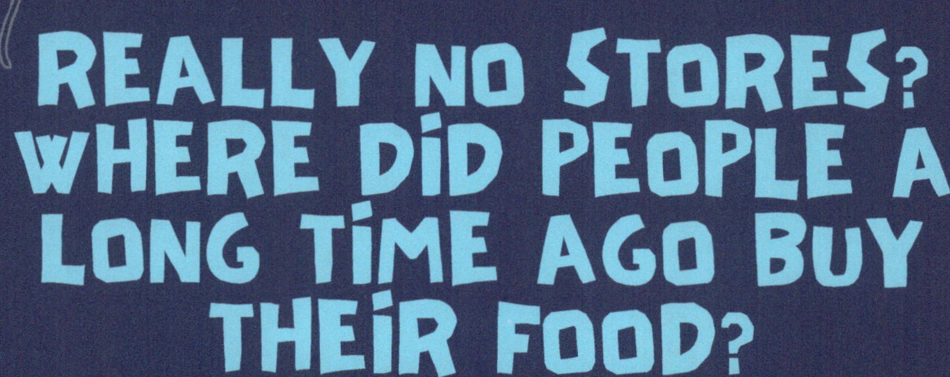

BTW. I'M TALKING ABOUT WHERE NORTHWEST U.S.A. IS TODAY

BTW 2. THAT ON TOP? IS NOT REAL FOOD!

A LONG TIME AGO
PEOPLE GATHERED
THEIR FOOD
FROM PLANTS,
AND HUNTED TOO

BUT
A LONG
TIME AGO THEY
ATE LOTS OF...

FiSH
AND SEALS AND
EVEN WHALES!
NOW THAT'S REAL FOOD!
PEOPLE A LONG TIME AGO ALSO
BELIEVED SALMONS WERE
SUPERNATURAL BEINGS

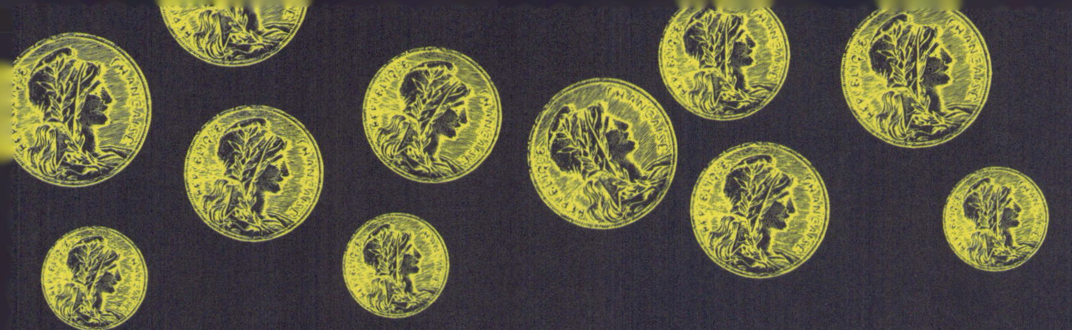

THAT IS WHY CHIEF SEALTH, WHO LIVED A LONG TIME AGO WHERE TODAY IS SEATTLE, WAS VERY SURPRISED WHEN PRESIDENT PIERCE OFFERED TO BUY THEIR LAND

BECAUSE, MAYBE YOU HAVE
ALREADY GUESSED,
THEY USED NO
MONEY

SEALTH: SEATTLE IN ENGLISH.
YES, THE CITY IS CALLED IN HIS HONOR.
DID YOU GUEST THAT?

THE EARTH IS
OUR MOTHER
AND THE RIVERS
OUR ANCESTORS
HE SAID
HOW CAN YOU BUY IT?
ANCESTORS: THE PARENTS
OF THE PARENTS OF THE
PARENTS OF THE PARENTS

THE DEAR,
THE BEAR,
THE EAGLE
ARE OUR BROTHERS

THE PERFUMED FLOWERS ARE OUR SISTERS.
EVERY PINE NEADLE IS SACRED TO US
THE MIST, THE DEW, THE ROCKY CREST ARE OUR FAMILY
HOW CAN YOU BUY IT?

Every Sandy Shore,
Every Humming Insect

Every Part of the Earth
is Sacred to Us

WE DONT OWN
THE FRESH AIR
OR THE CLEAR
WATER.

THIS WE KNOW: THE EARTH DOES NOT
BELONG TO MAN, MAN BELONGS TO THE
EARTH. ALL THINGS ARE CONNECTED.

WE ARE ALL CONNECTED
LIKE THREAD IS CONNECTED IN THIS FABRIC
EARTH, PLANTS, ANIMALS AND HUMAN ARE ONE
LET'S SAY YOU ARE THIS READ TREAD
IF SOMETHING HAPPENS TO YOU, IT HAPPENS TO ALL

FINALLY HE SAiD:

A LONG LONG TIME HAS PASSED SINCE....

NOWADAYS WE HAVE

ICE CREAM!

THAT'S SO GOOD!

BUT I WANT TO ASK YOU SOMETHING...

NO, IT'S NOT TO EAT THAT GREEN SCOOP

PLEASE SAY HELLO TO OUR FAMILY EVERY TIME YOU CAN
PLAY WITH THE WIND
OBSERVE ANIMALS, BIRDS AND INSECTS
SMELL THE FLOWERS
HUG A TREE

CHIEF SEATTLE
WOULD BY
So HAPPY!

THIS PAGE IS MY PRESENT, SO YOU CAN COLOR IT
I'M SUPERNATURAL!
YES, YOU ARE!

HERE YOU CAN PAINT ANYTHING YOU WANT. I STAR:
FINALLY! I HAVE WANTED TO USE THIS SHE SUN SINCE THE BEGINNING
AND HERE YOU GO!

MY NAME IS LILAH AND WHAT I LOVE THE MOST IS TO READ AND WRITE. MY DAUGHTER WHO WAS BORN IN 2014 IT A GREAT INSPIRATION AND HELPS ME WITH THE SELECTION OF THE IMAGES. THANKS TO THE PROGRAM CANVA WE CAN BEAUTIFULLY ILLUSTRATE THE MANY STORIES WE WANT TO SHARE!

I HOPE YOU KEEP READING BECAUSE I THINK IT IS ONE OF THE BEST THINGS IN THE WORLD! MAKES ME HAPPY WHEN I'M SAD AND MAKES ME TRAVEL WHEN I'M AT HOME TO LANDS FAR, FAR AWAY, TO TIMES LONG, LONG AGO AND TO WORDS THAT ONLY EXIST IN THE IMAGINATION.

I'M WEARING AN AFRICAN SCARF IN MY PICTURE HERE BECAUSE I LIVED THERE A FEW YEARS, WHEN I MEET AMARA, WHO IS A AMAZING PERSON THAT HAS BROUGHT A LOT OF JOY AND LOVE TO MY LIFE, AS YOU CAN PROBABLY SEE ON THE BACK COVER PICTURE.

IF YOU HAVE ANY QUESTION TO US, WE WOULD BE VERY HAPPY TO ANSWER ALL OF THEM. PLEASE WRITE TO US AT alraiti@hotmail.com.

UNTIL NEXT TIME, HAPPY READING!